Josef
SUK

POHÁDKA LÉTA
A Summer Tale
Op. 29
(1908)

Study Score

SERENISSIMA MUSIC, INC.

INSTRUMENTATION

3 Flutes (3 doubles Piccolo)
2 Oboes (2 doubles English Horn)
English Horn
3 Clarinets in A (3 doubles Bass Clarinet in A)
2 Bassoons
Contrabassoon

6 Horns in F (4-6 also in D)
3 Trumpets in C
3 Trombones
Tuba

Timpani
Percussion
(Triangle, Tam-Tam, Cymbals, Bass Drum)
Organ (ad lib.)
Piano
Celesta
2 Harps

Violin I
Violin II
Viola
Violoncello
Bass

Duration: ca. 50 minutes

Premiere
Prague: January 26, 1909
Czech Philharmonic Orchestra
Karel Kovarovic, conductor

ISBN: 1-932419-59-4

This score is a slightly modified unabridged reprint of the
score published in 1910 by Universal Edition, Vienna.
The score has been reduced to fit the present format.

Printed in the USA
First Printing: Ocober, 2007

Karlu Kovařovicovi

POHÁDKA LÉTA
(A SUMMER TALE)

I. Hlasy Života a Útěchy
(Voices of Life and Consolation)

Josef Suk, Op. 29

SERENISSIMA MUSIC, INC.

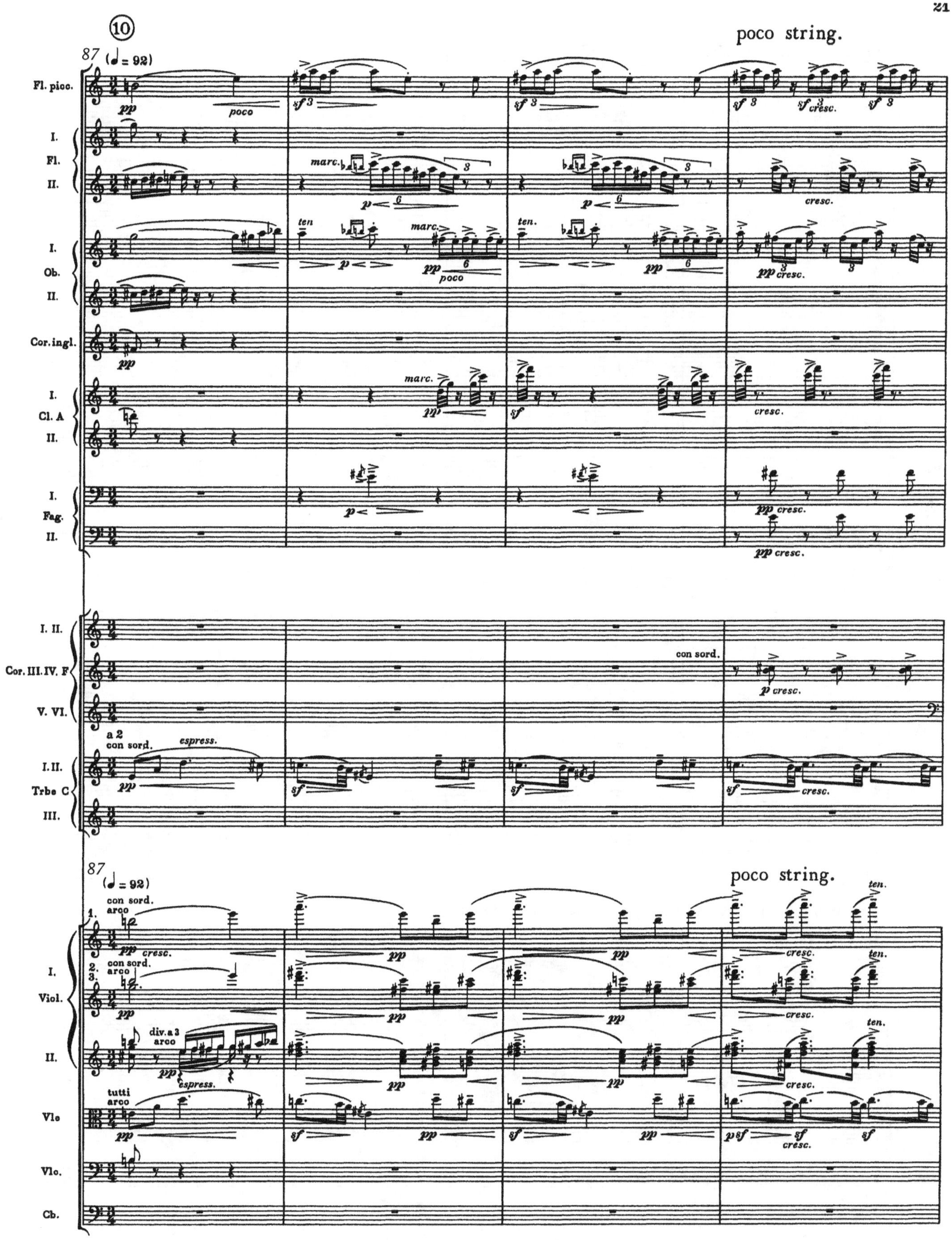
10
87
(𝅗𝅥 = 92)
poco string.
Fl. picc.
I. Fl. II.
I. Ob. II.
Cor. ingl.
I. Cl. A II.
I. Fag. II.
I. II. Cor. III. IV. F V. VI.
I. II. Trbe C III.
Viol. I.
II.
Vle
Vlc.
Cb.
pp
poco
sf
cresc.
marc.
ten.
p
con sord.
a 2
espress.
arco
div. a 3
tutti

22

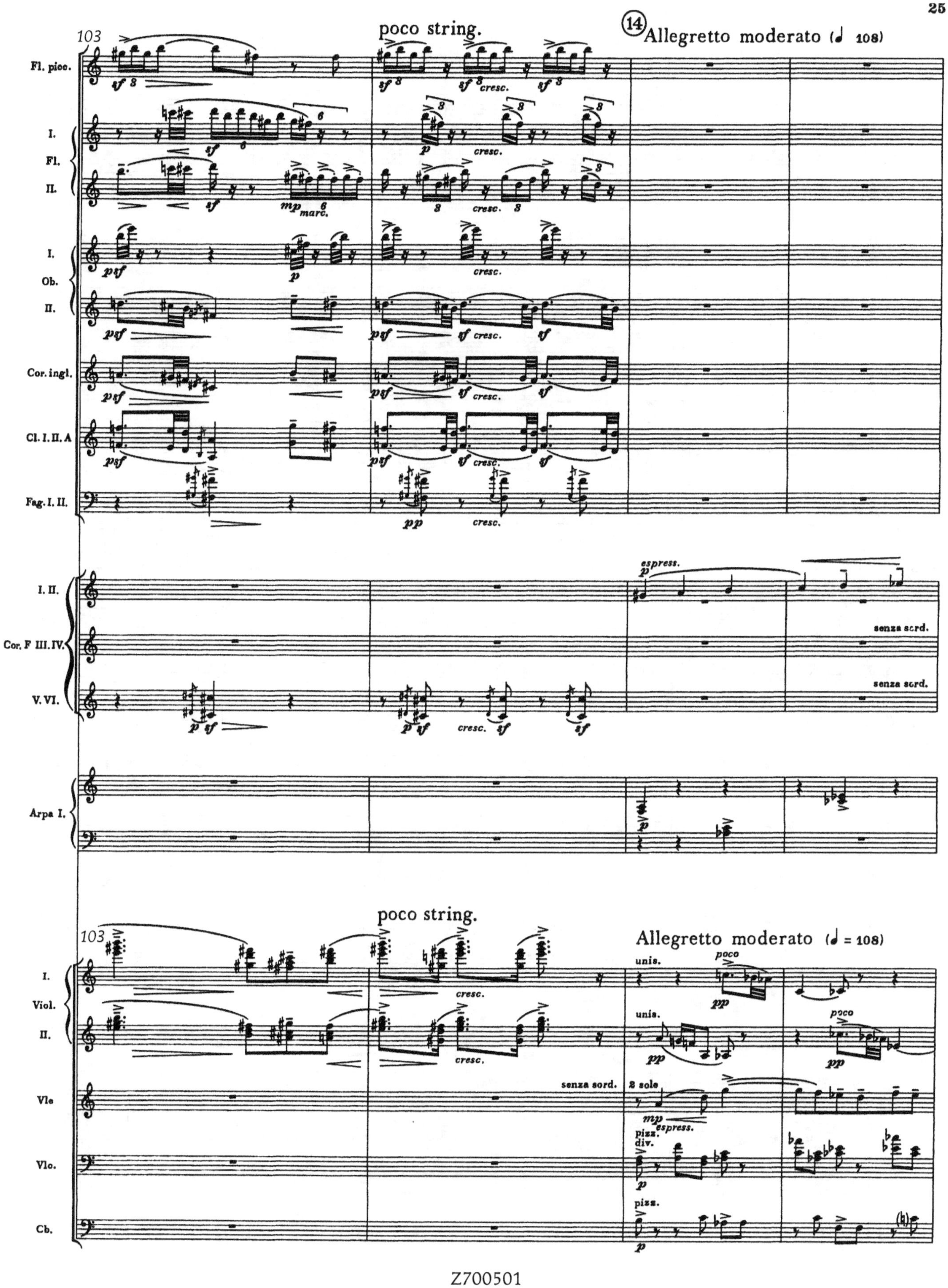
103
poco string.
14
Allegretto moderato (♩ 108)
Fl. picc.
I.
Fl.
II.
I.
Ob.
II.
Cor. ingl.
Cl. I. II. A
Fag. I. II.
I. II.
Cor. F III. IV.
V. VI.
espress.
senza sord.
senza sord.
Arpa I.
103
poco string.
Allegretto moderato (♩ = 108)
I.
Viol.
II.
unis.
unis.
poco
Vle
senza sord.
2 sole
espress.
Vlc.
pizz.
div.
Cb.
pizz.
cresc.
marc.

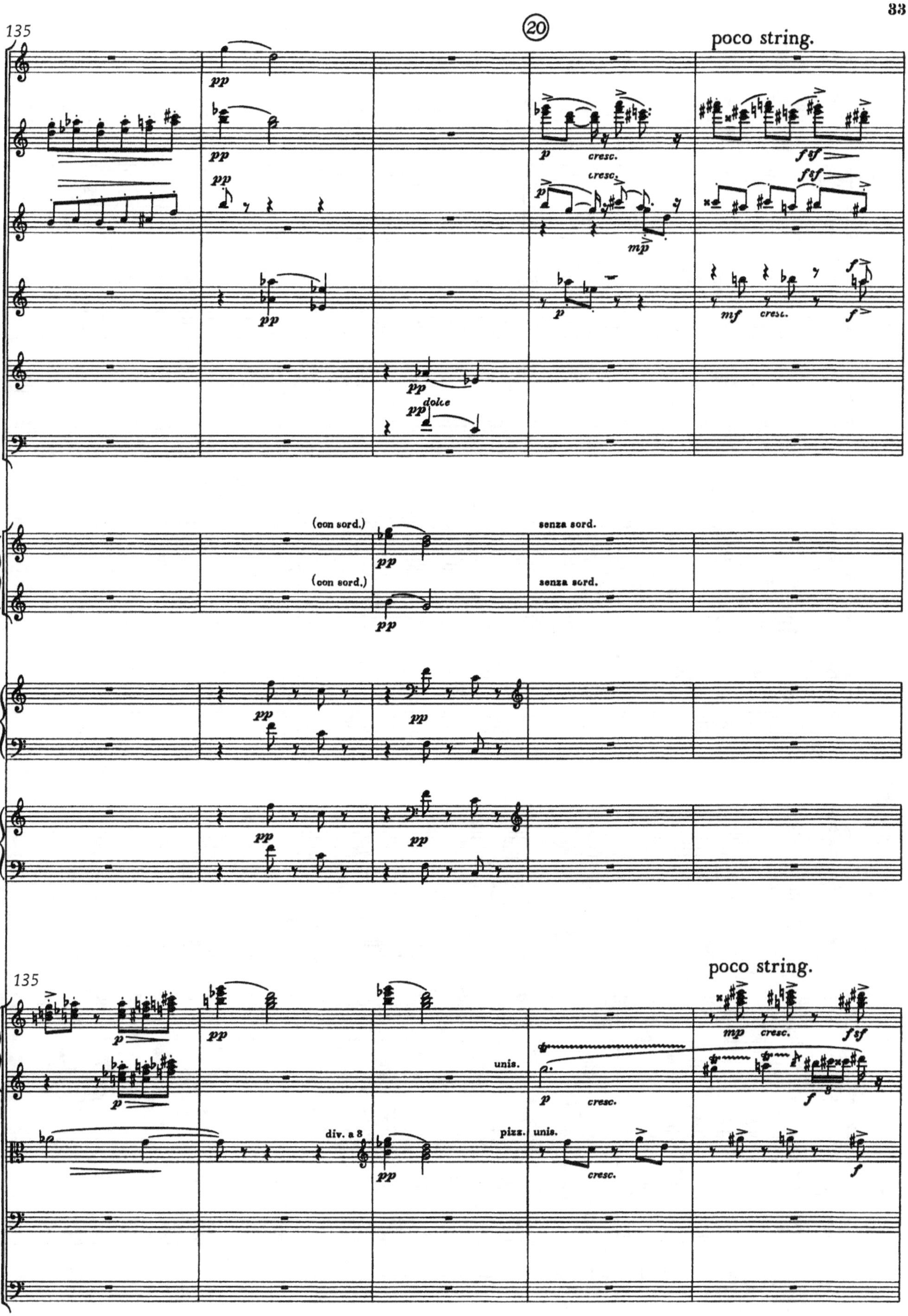
135
20
poco string.
Fl. picc.
Fl. I. II.
Ob. I. II.
Cl. I. II. A
Cl. basso A
Fag. I. II.
pp
p
cresc.
fsf
mp
mf
f
dolce
(con sord.)
senza sord.
I. II.
Trbe C
III.
Arpa I.
Arpa II.
135
poco string.
I.
Viol.
II.
unis.
div. a 3
pizz.
Vle
Vlc.
Cb.

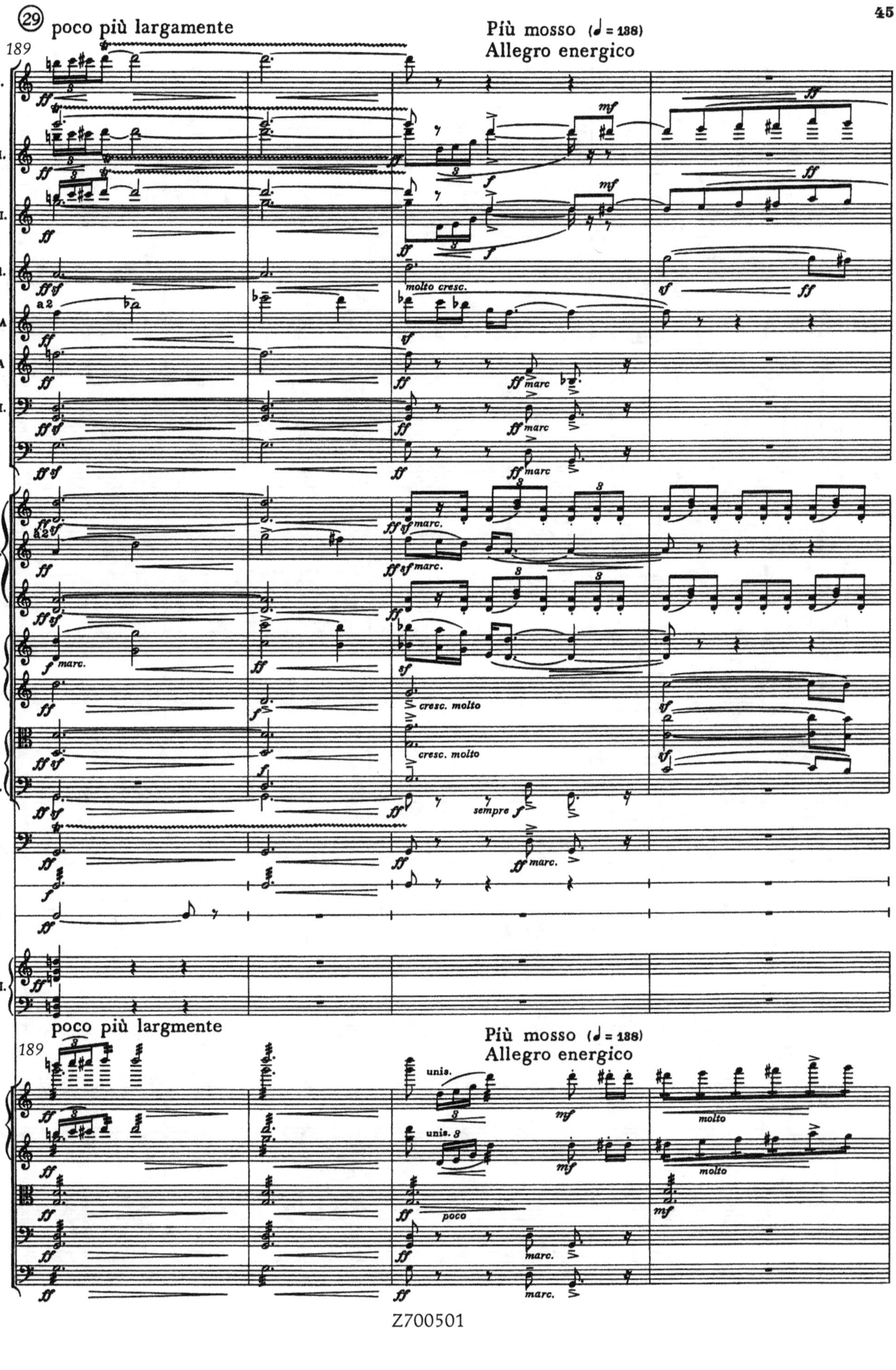
29
poco più largamente
189
Più mosso (♩ = 138)
Allegro energico
Fl. picc.
Fl. I. II.
Ob. I. II.
Cor. ingl.
molto cresc.
Cl. I. II. A
a 2
Cl. basso A
marc
Fag. I. II.
Cfag.
I. II.
Cor. F III. IV.
V. VI.
marc.
I. II.
Trbe C
III.
cresc. molto
I. II.
Trbni
III. e Tb.
sempre
Timp.
Trgl.
Piatti
Arpa I. II.
poco più largmente
189
Più mosso (♩ = 138)
Allegro energico
unis.
I.
Viol.
II.
molto
Vle
poco
Vlc.
Cb.

46

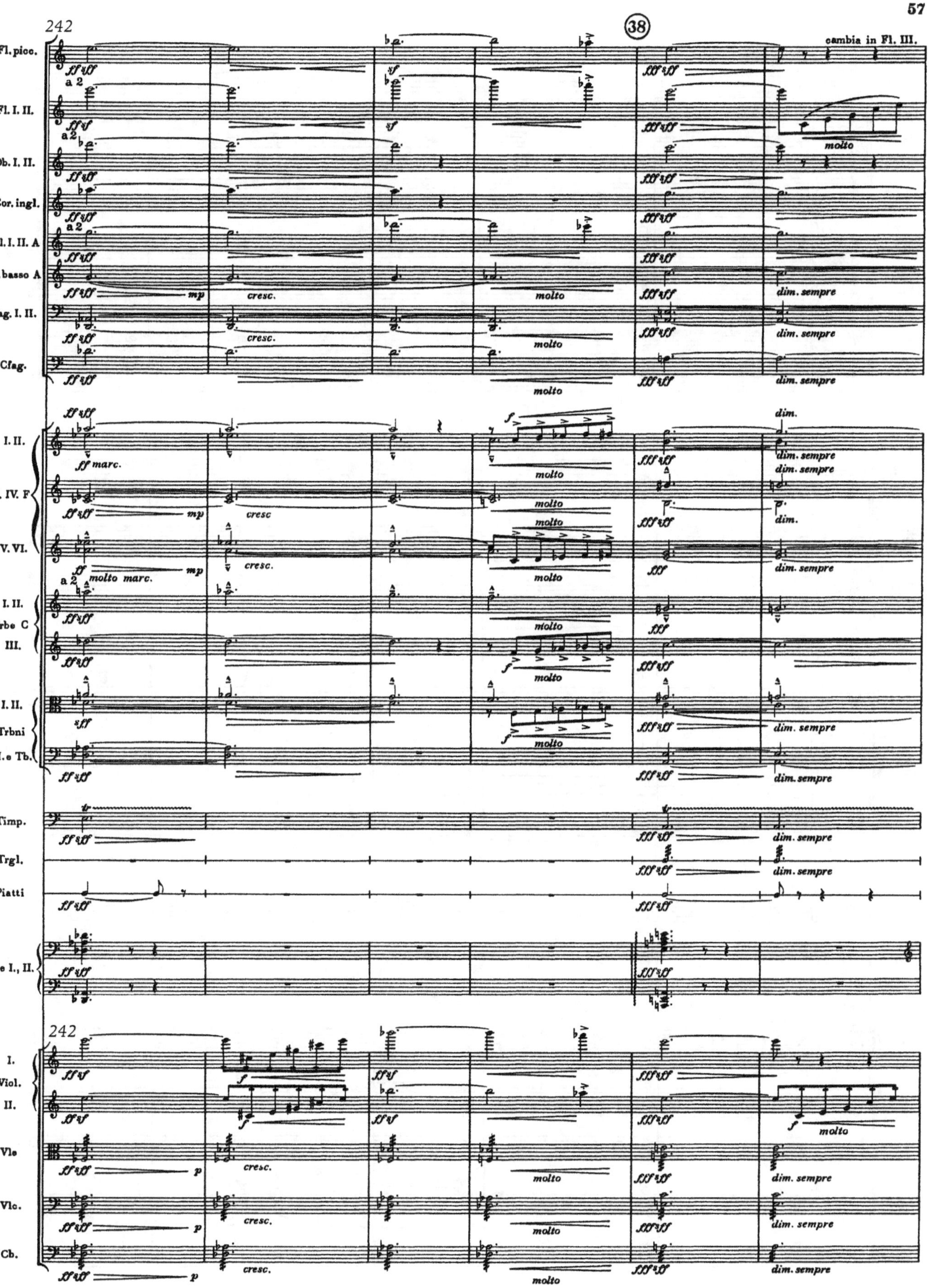

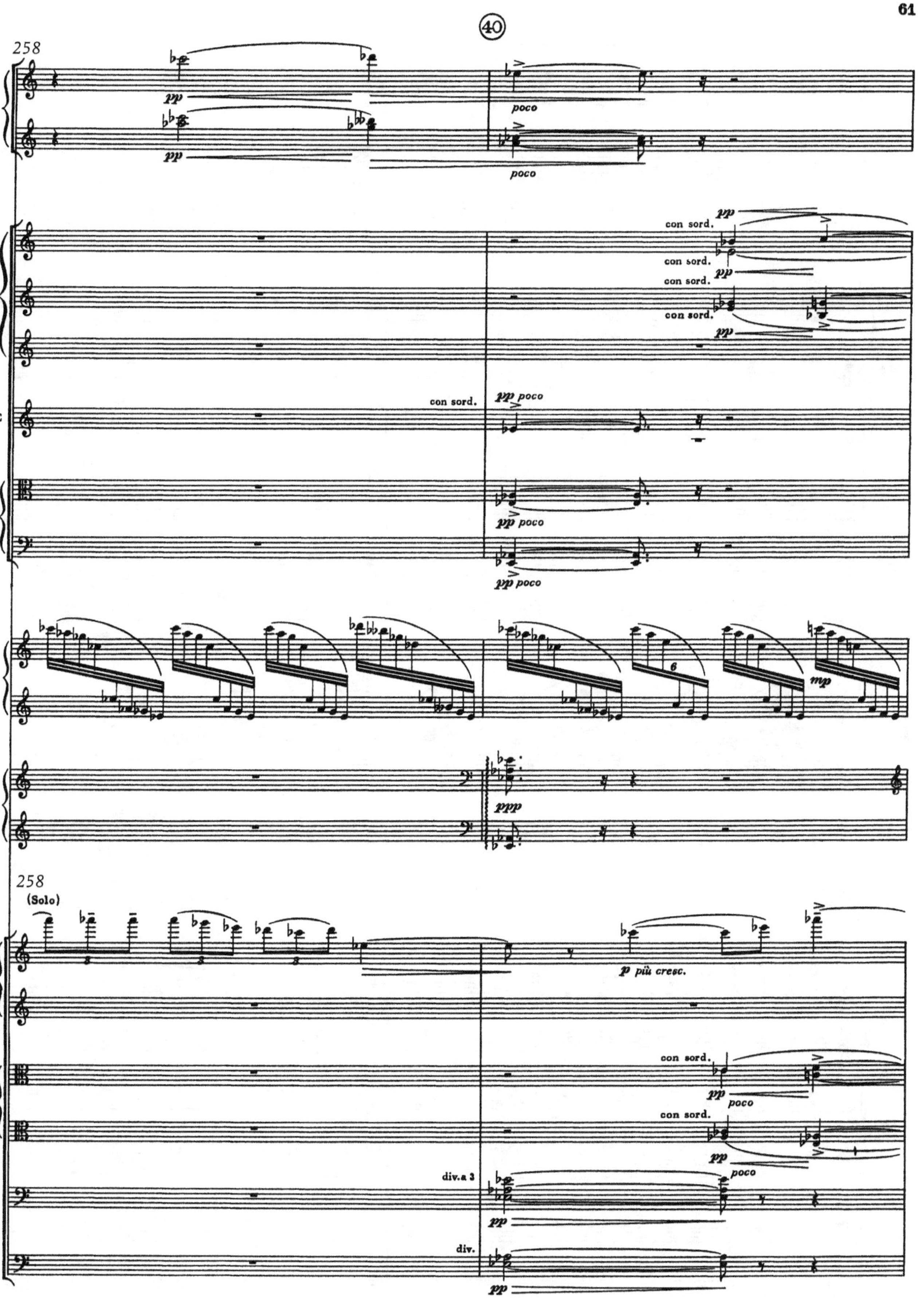
40
258
III.
Fl.
I. II.
pp
poco
I. II.
Cor. III.IV. F
V. VI.
con sord.
Trbe I.II. C
I.II.
Trbni
III. e Tb.
pp poco
Arpa I.
mp
Arpa II.
ppp
258
(Solo)
I.
Viol.
II.
p più cresc.
1.
2.
Vle
(div. a 4)
3.
4.
Vlc.
div. a 3
Cb.
div.

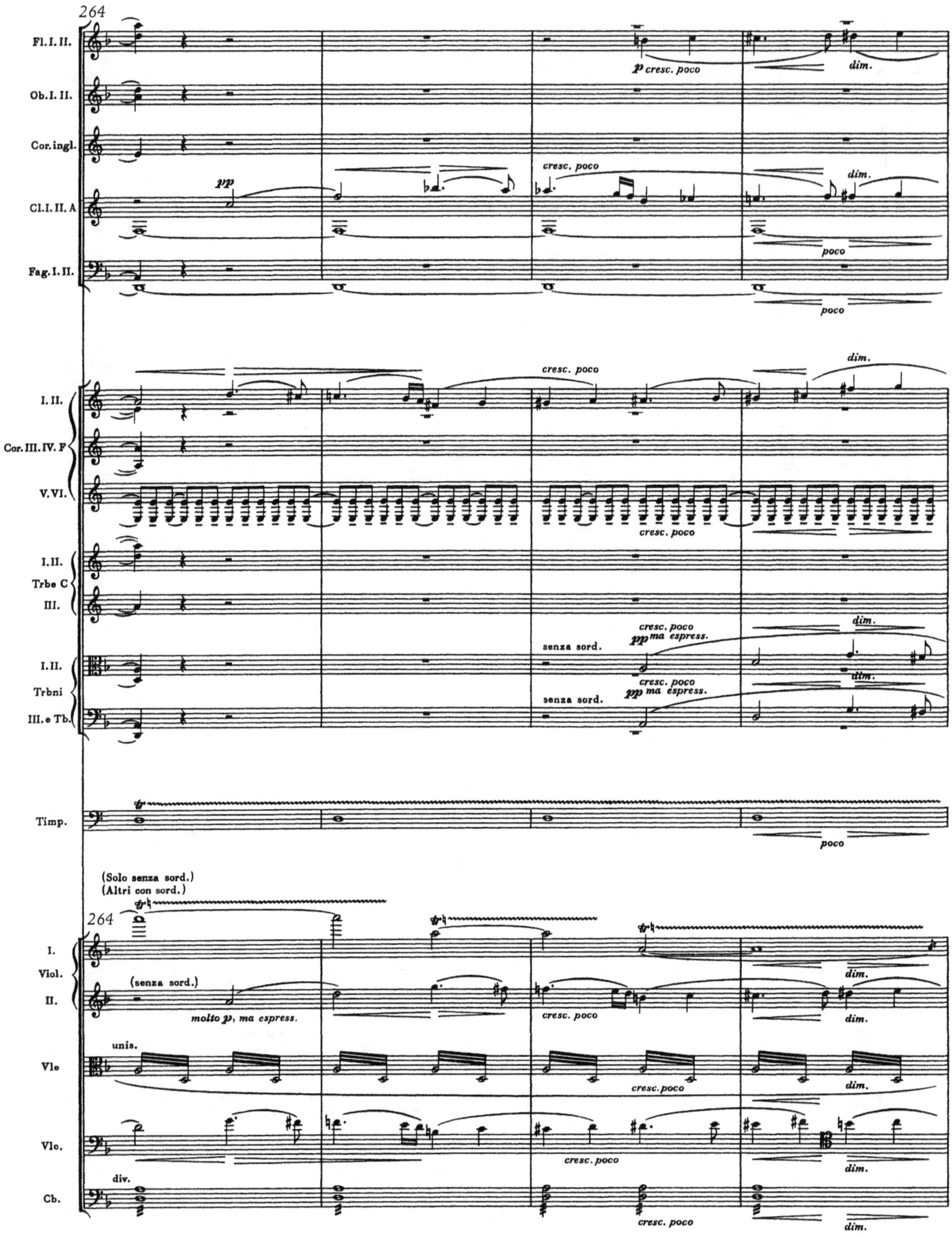
264
Fl. I. II.
Ob. I. II.
Cor. ingl.
Cl. I. II. A
Fag. I. II.
I. II.
Cor. III. IV. F
V. VI.
I. II.
Trbe C
III.
I. II.
Trbni
III. e Tb.
Timp.
I.
Viol.
II.
Vle
Vlc.
Cb.
p cresc. poco
dim.
pp
cresc. poco
poco
senza sord.
cresc. poco
pp ma espress.
(Solo senza sord.)
(Altri con sord.)
(senza sord.)
molto p, ma espress.
unis.
div.

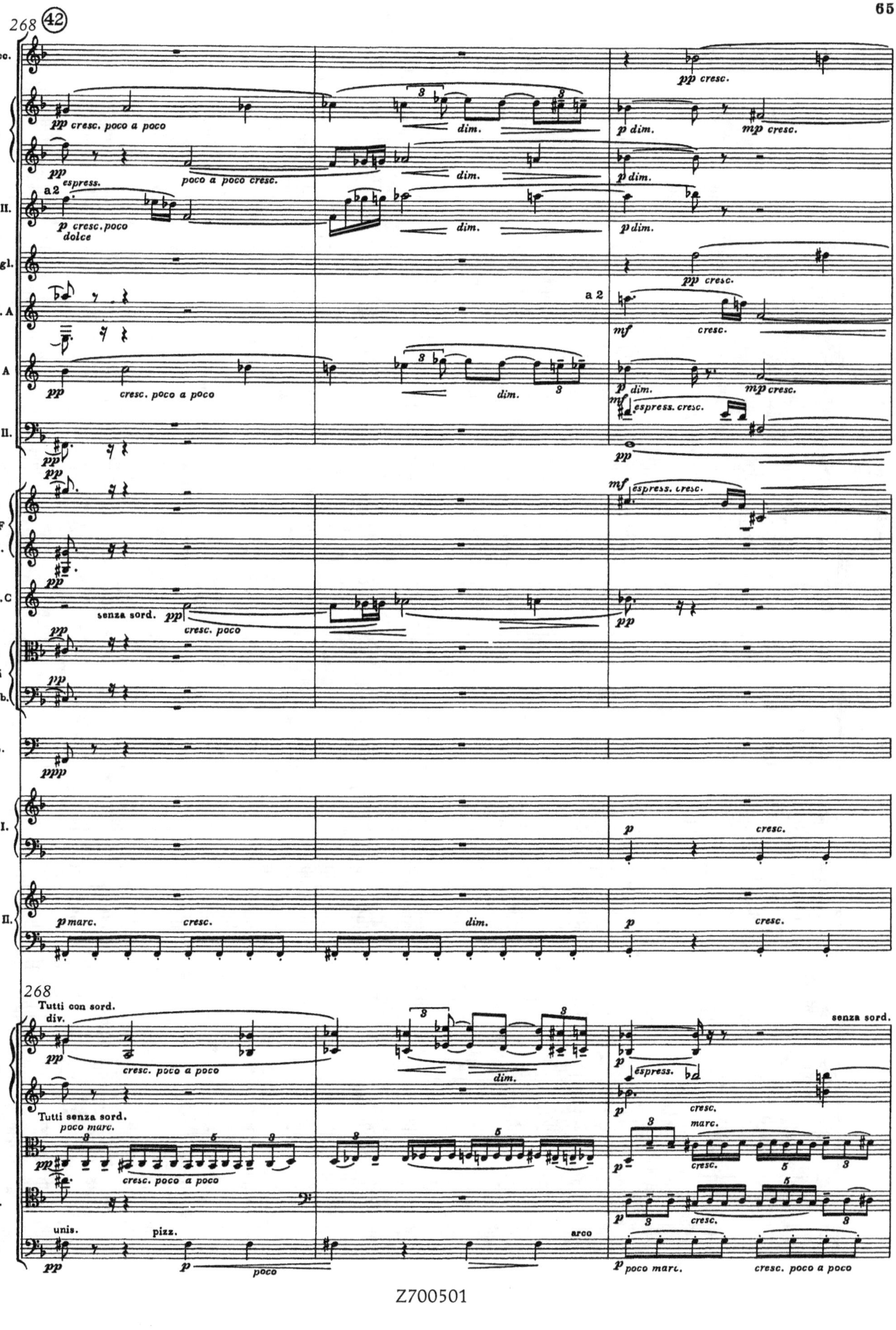
268
42
Fl. picc.
I.
Fl.
II.
Ob. I. II.
Cor. ingl.
Cl. I. II. A
Cl. basso A
Fag. I. II.
I. II.
Cor. F
V. VI.
Trbe I. II. C
I. II.
Trbni
III. e Tb.
Timp.
Arpa I.
Arpa II.
I.
Viol.
II.
Vle
Vlc.
Cb.
pp cresc. poco a poco
pp espress.
poco a poco cresc.
a 2
p cresc. poco dolce
dim.
p dim.
mp cresc.
pp cresc.
mf
espress. cresc.
senza sord.
cresc. poco
ppp
p marc.
cresc.
Tutti con sord.
div.
Tutti senza sord.
poco marc.
unis.
pizz.
arco
poco
espress.
marc.
p poco marc.
cresc. poco a poco

*) con dolcezza, ma chiaramente fino al fine.

II. Poledne
(Midday)

*) Dopo i primi due quarti di ogni battuta staccare un pó.

78

82

*) Dirigere in due battute divise in quarti.

Z700501

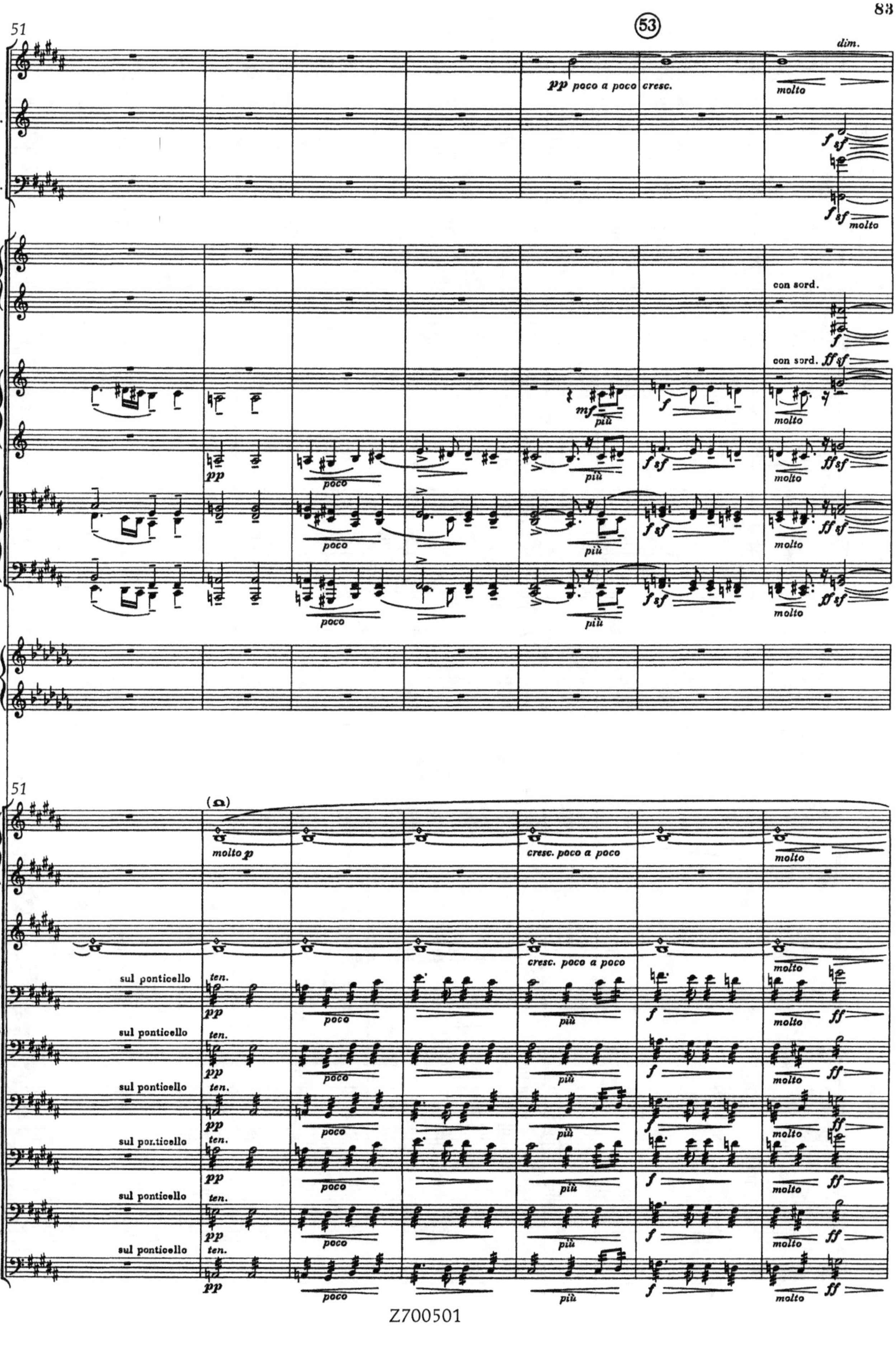
51
53
Fl. picc.
pp poco a poco cresc.
dim.
molto
Cor. ingl.
Fag. I. II.
f sf
molto
I. II.
Cor. F
III. IV.
con sord.
I. II.
Trbe C
III.
mf
più
poco
pp
ff sf
Trbni
III. e Tb.
Arpe I., II.
I.
Viol.
II.
Vle
molto p
cresc. poco a poco
sul ponticello
ten.
Vlc. (div.)
Cb. (div.)
ff

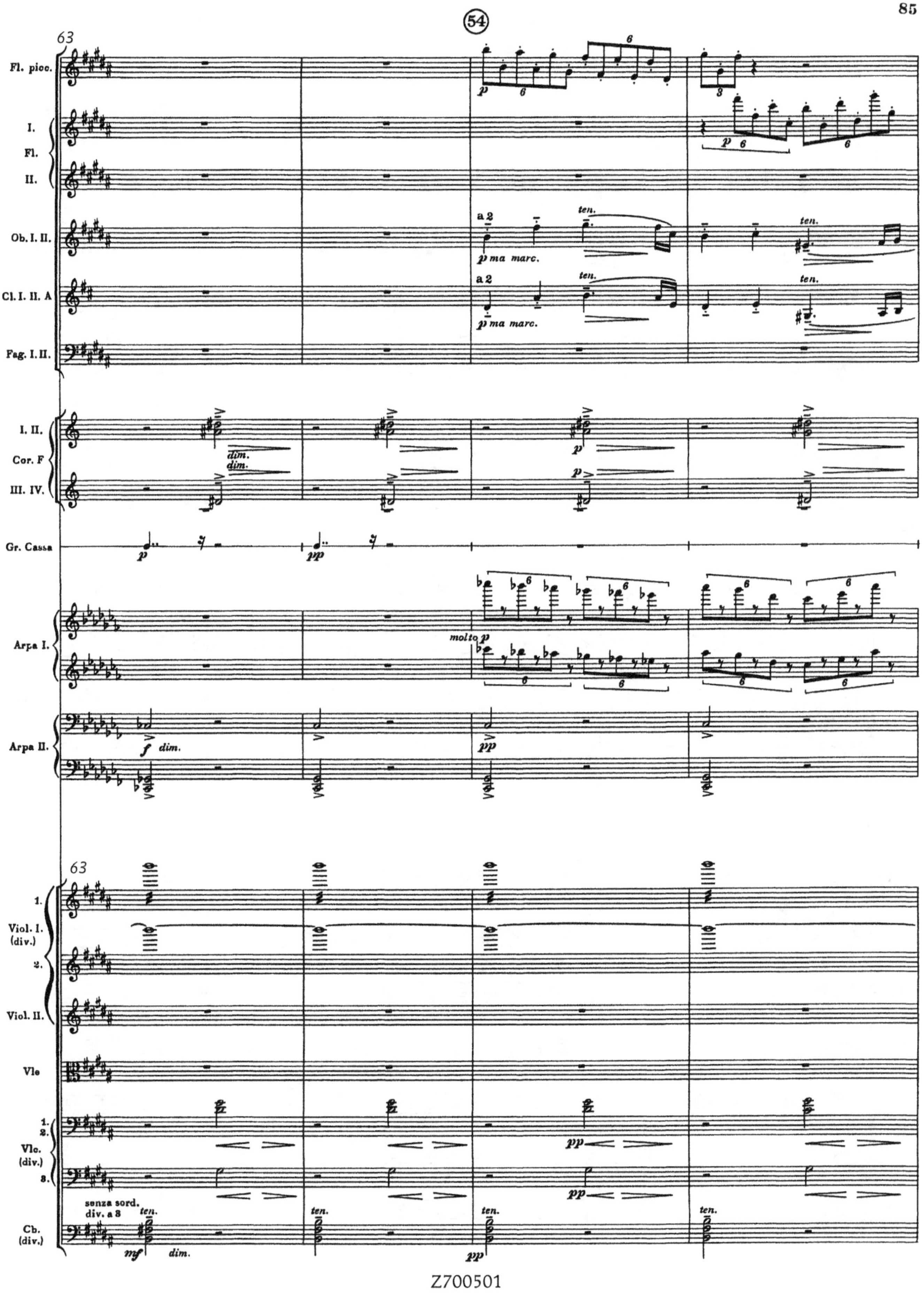
54
63
Fl. picc.
I.
Fl.
II.
Ob. I. II.
Cl. I. II. A
Fag. I. II.
I. II.
Cor. F
III. IV.
Gr. Cassa
Arpa I.
Arpa II.
Viol. I. (div.)
Viol. II.
Vle
Vlc. (div.)
Cb. (div.)
a 2
p ma marc.
ten.
dim.
molto p
f dim.
senza sord.
div. a 3
mf dim.
pp

86

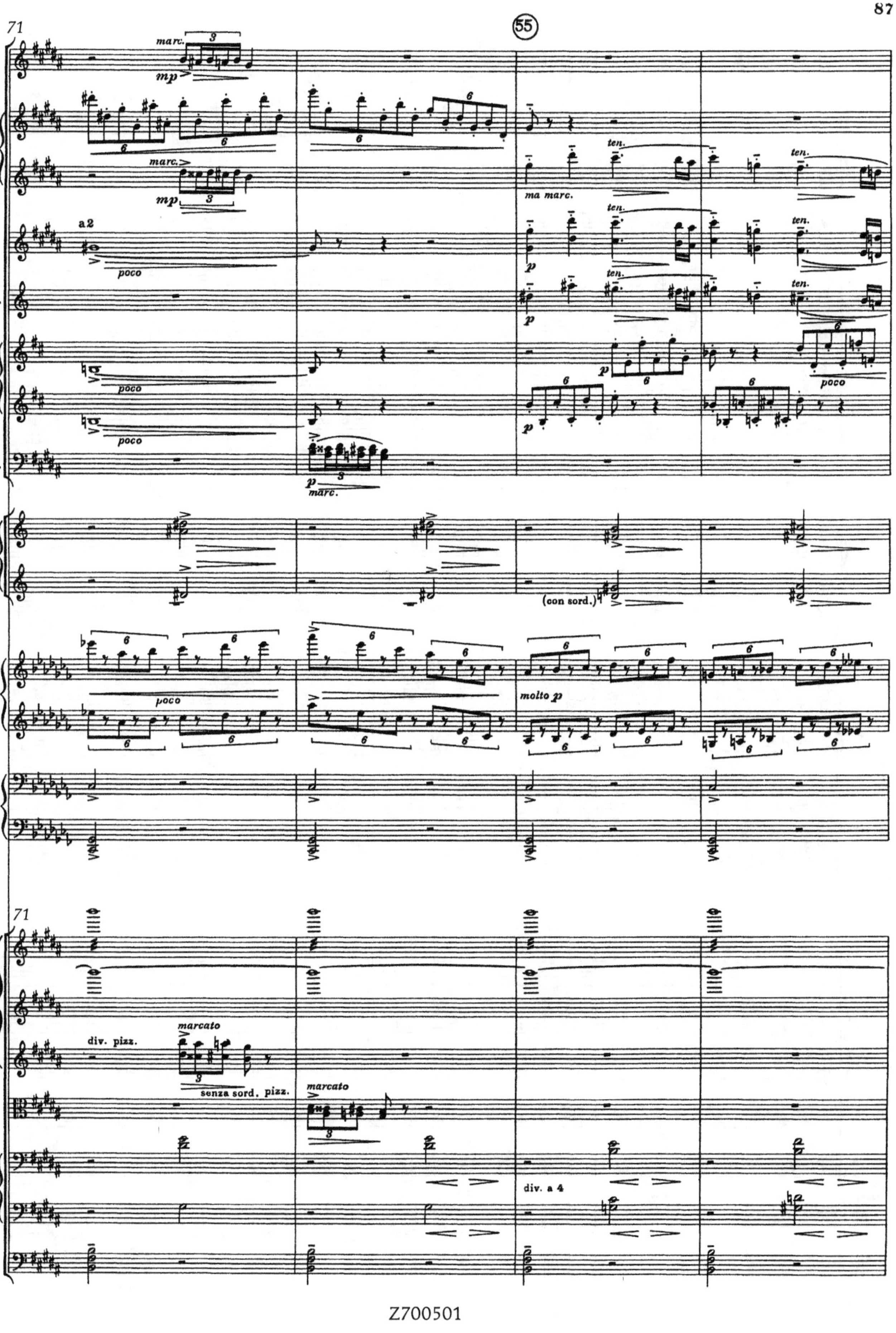
71
55
Fl. picc.
Fl. I.
Fl. II.
Ob. I. II.
Cor. ingl.
Cl. A I.
Cl. A II.
Fag. I. II.
Cor. F I. II.
Cor. F III. IV.
Arpa I.
Arpa II.
Viol. I. (div.) 1.
Viol. I. (div.) 2.
Viol. II.
Vle
Vlc. (div.) 1. 2.
Vlc. (div.) 3.
Cb. (div.)
marc.
mp
ma marc.
ten.
a 2
poco
p
marc.
(con sord.)
molto p
div. pizz.
marcato
senza sord. pizz.
div. a 4

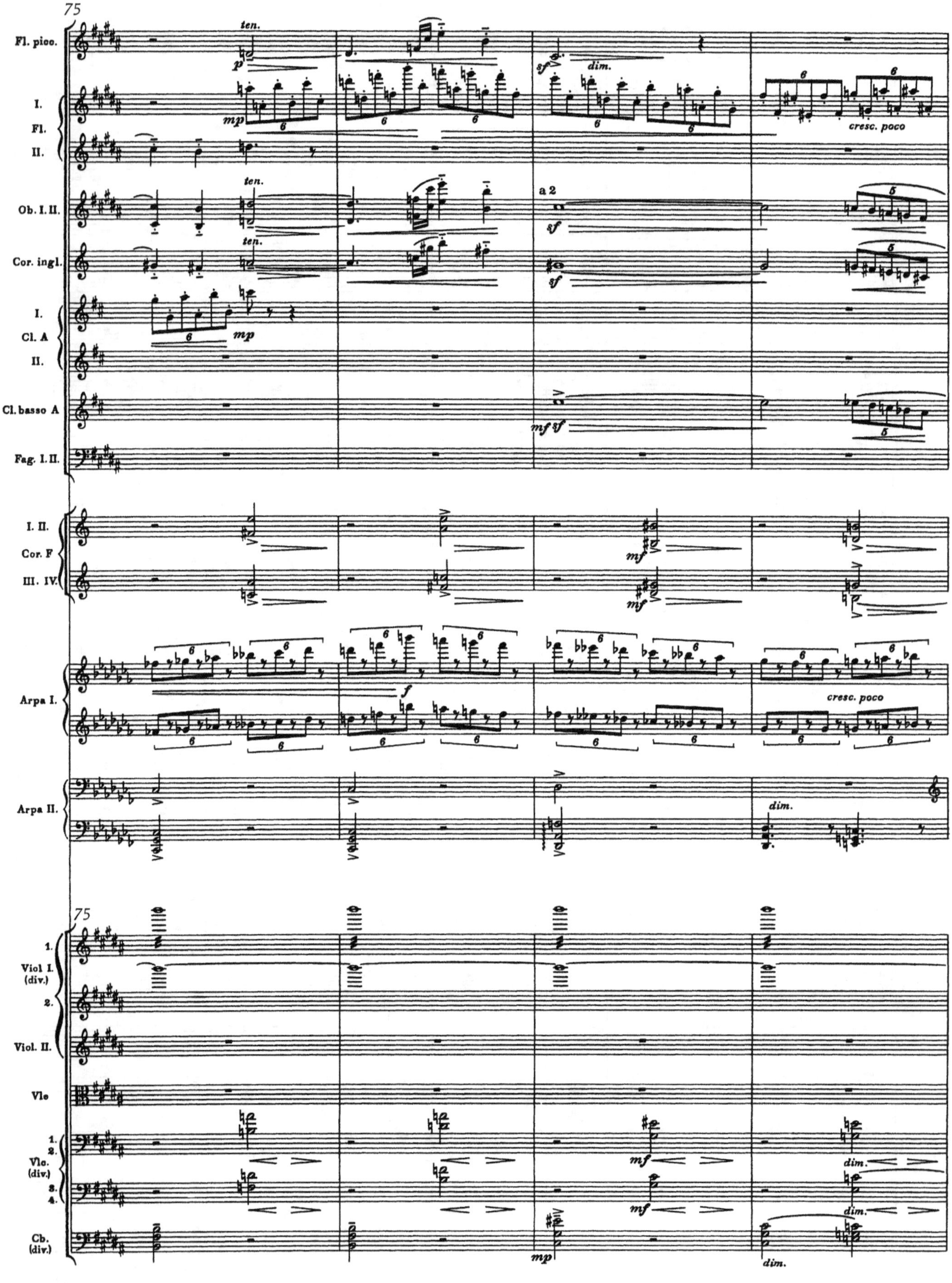
75
Fl. picc.
ten.
p
sf
dim.
I.
Fl.
II.
mp
cresc. poco
Ob. I. II.
a 2
sf
Cor. ingl.
I.
Cl. A
II.
Cl. basso A
mf sf
Fag. I. II.
I. II.
Cor. F
III. IV.
mf
Arpa I.
f
Arpa II.
dim.
75
Viol I. (div.)
Viol. II.
Vle
Vlc. (div.)
Cb. (div.)
mp

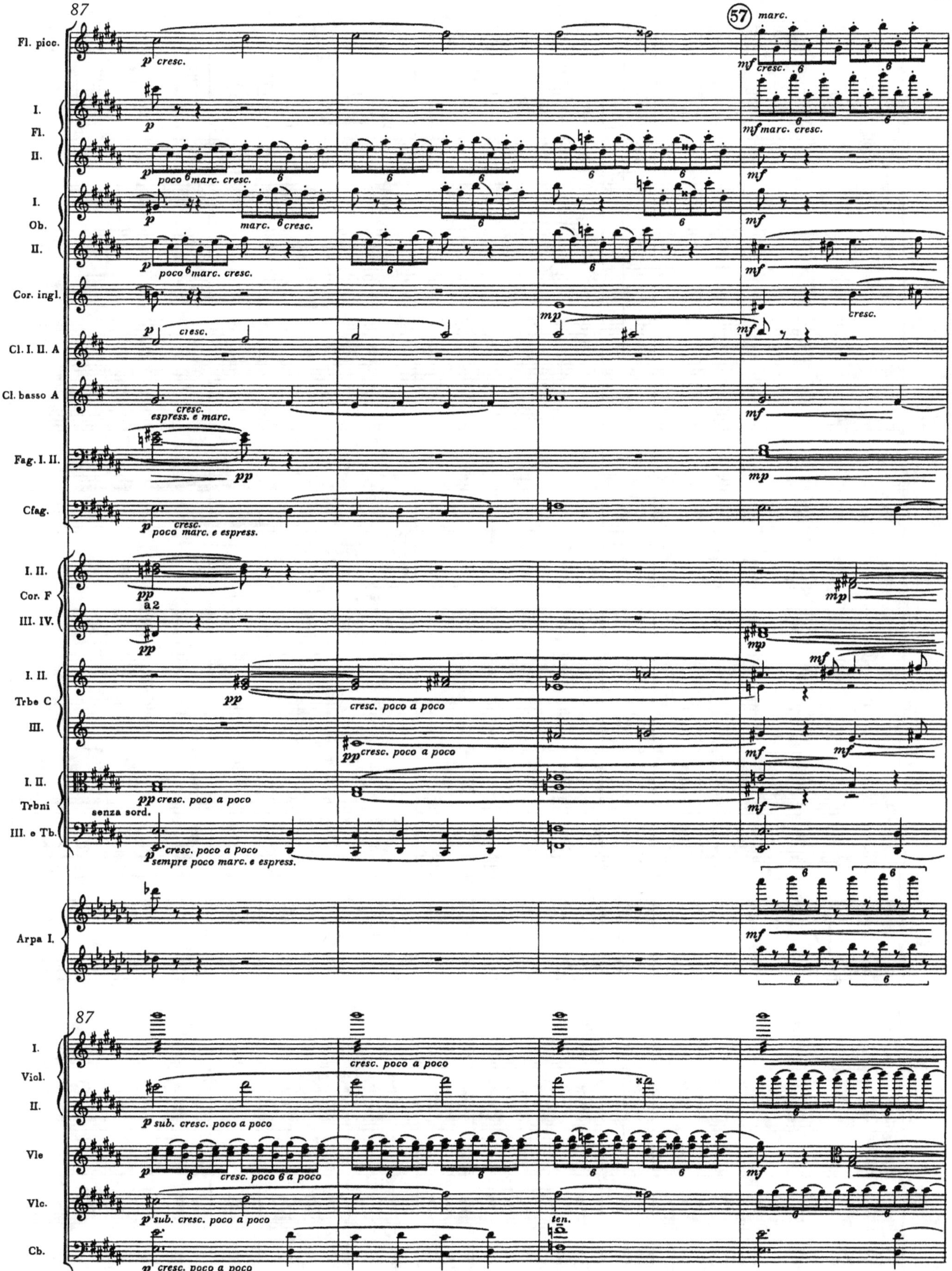
87
57
Fl. picc.
I. Fl. II.
I. Ob. II.
Cor. ingl.
Cl. I. II. A
Cl. basso A
Fag. I. II.
Cfag.
I. II. Cor. F III. IV.
I. II. Trbe C III.
I. II. Trbni III. e Tb.
Arpa I.
I. Viol. II.
Vle
Vlc.
Cb.
marc.
cresc.
poco marc. cresc.
marc. cresc.
espress. e marc.
poco marc. e espress.
a 2
cresc. poco a poco
senza sord.
sempre poco marc. e espress.
p sub. cresc. poco a poco
ten.

92

94

III. Intermezzo – Slepí Hudci
(Intermezzo – Blind Musicians)

IV. V Moci Přeludů
(In the Power of Phantoms)

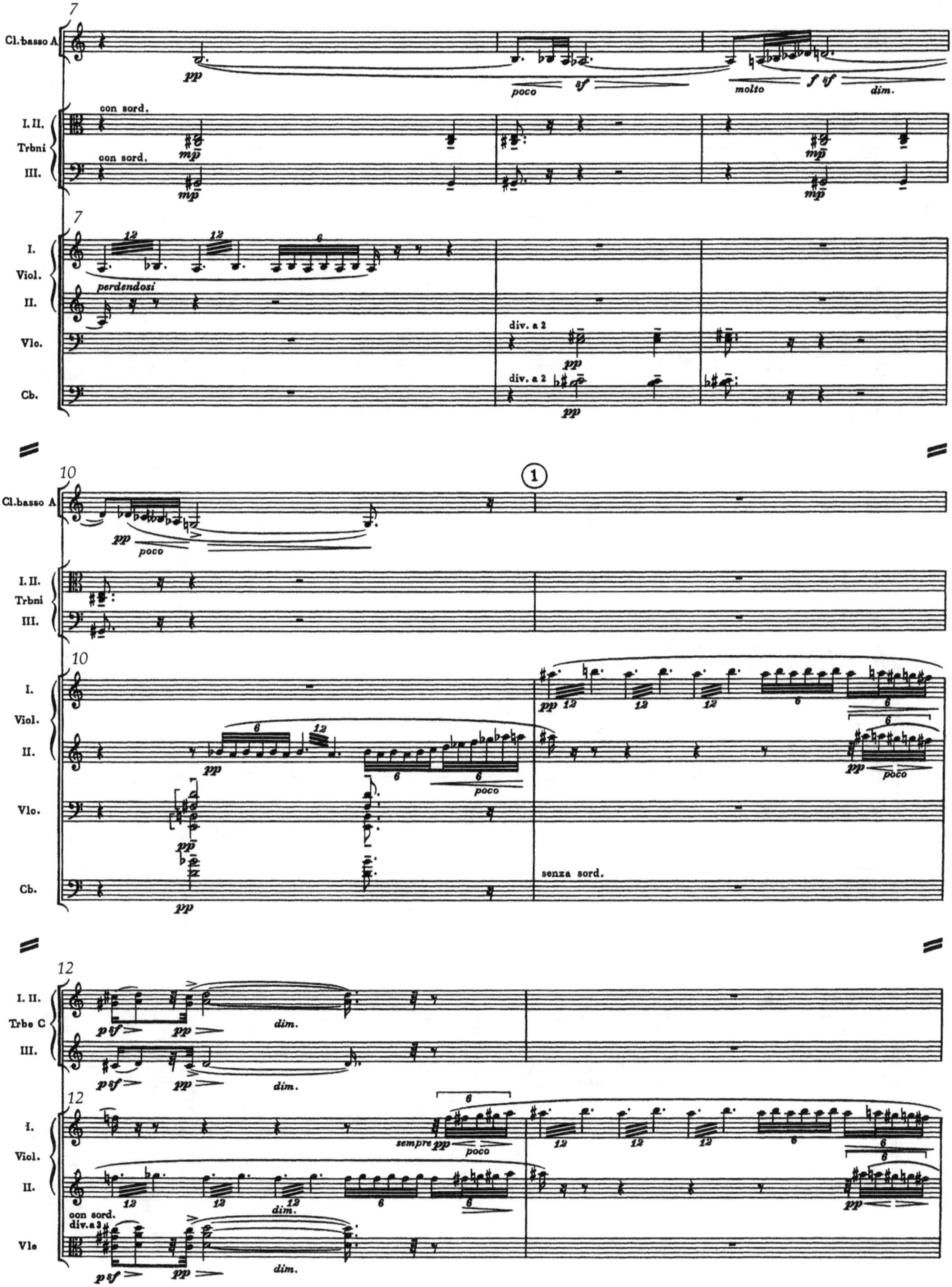
Cl. basso A
I. II.
Trbni
III.
con sord.
I.
Viol.
II.
Vlc.
Cb.
perdendosi
div. a 2
poco
molto
dim.
senza sord.
I. II.
Trbe C
III.
Vle
con sord.
div. a 3
sempre
1

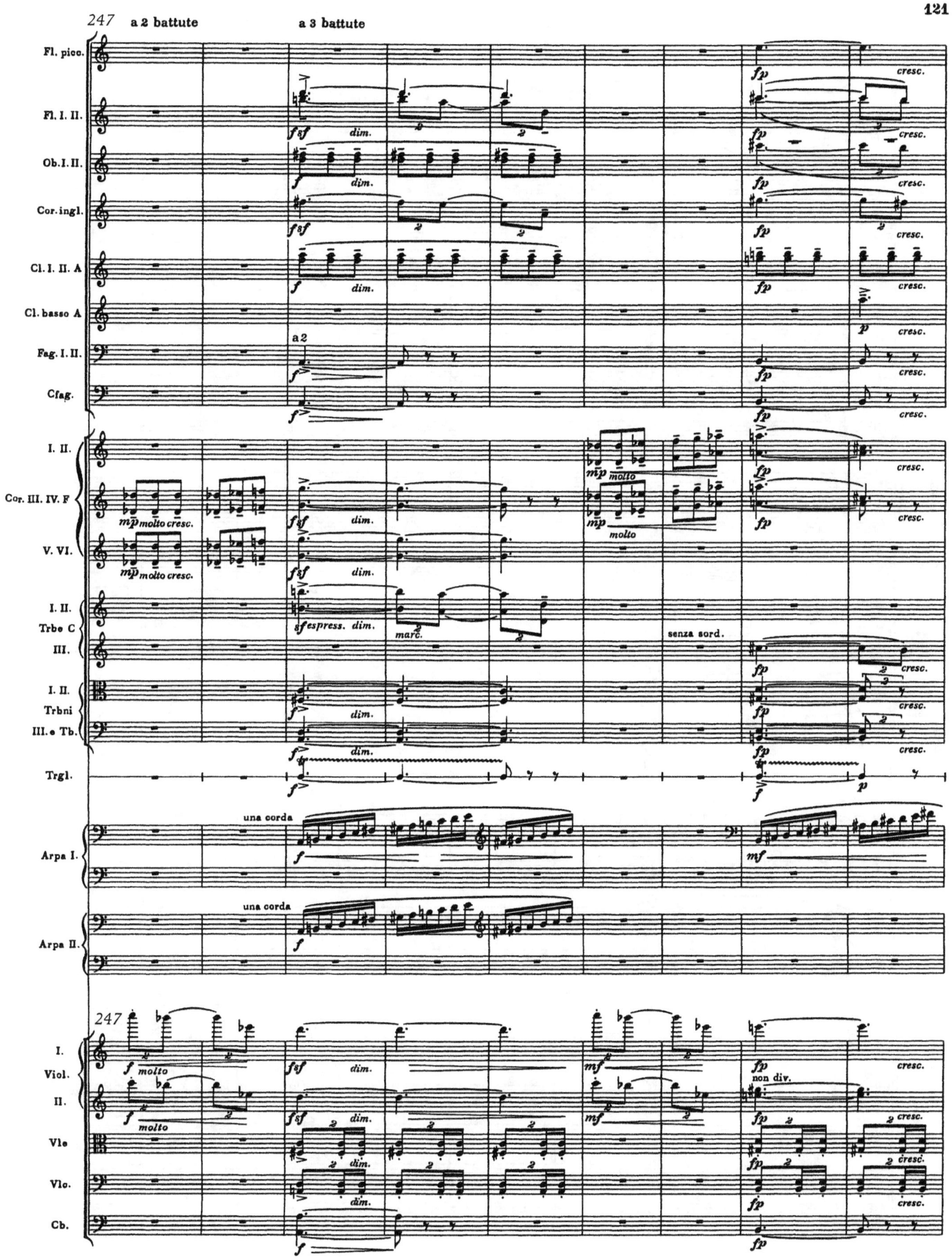
247
a 2 battute
a 3 battute
Fl. picc.
Fl. I. II.
Ob. I. II.
Cor. ingl.
Cl. I. II. A
Cl. basso A
Fag. I. II.
Cfag.
Cor. III. IV. F
I. II.
V. VI.
Trbe C
I. II.
III.
Trbni
I. II.
III. e Tb.
Trgl.
Arpa I.
Arpa II.
Viol.
I.
II.
Vle
Vlc.
Cb.
fsf
dim.
cresc.
fp
molto cresc.
molto
espress. dim.
marc.
senza sord.
una corda
non div.
a 2

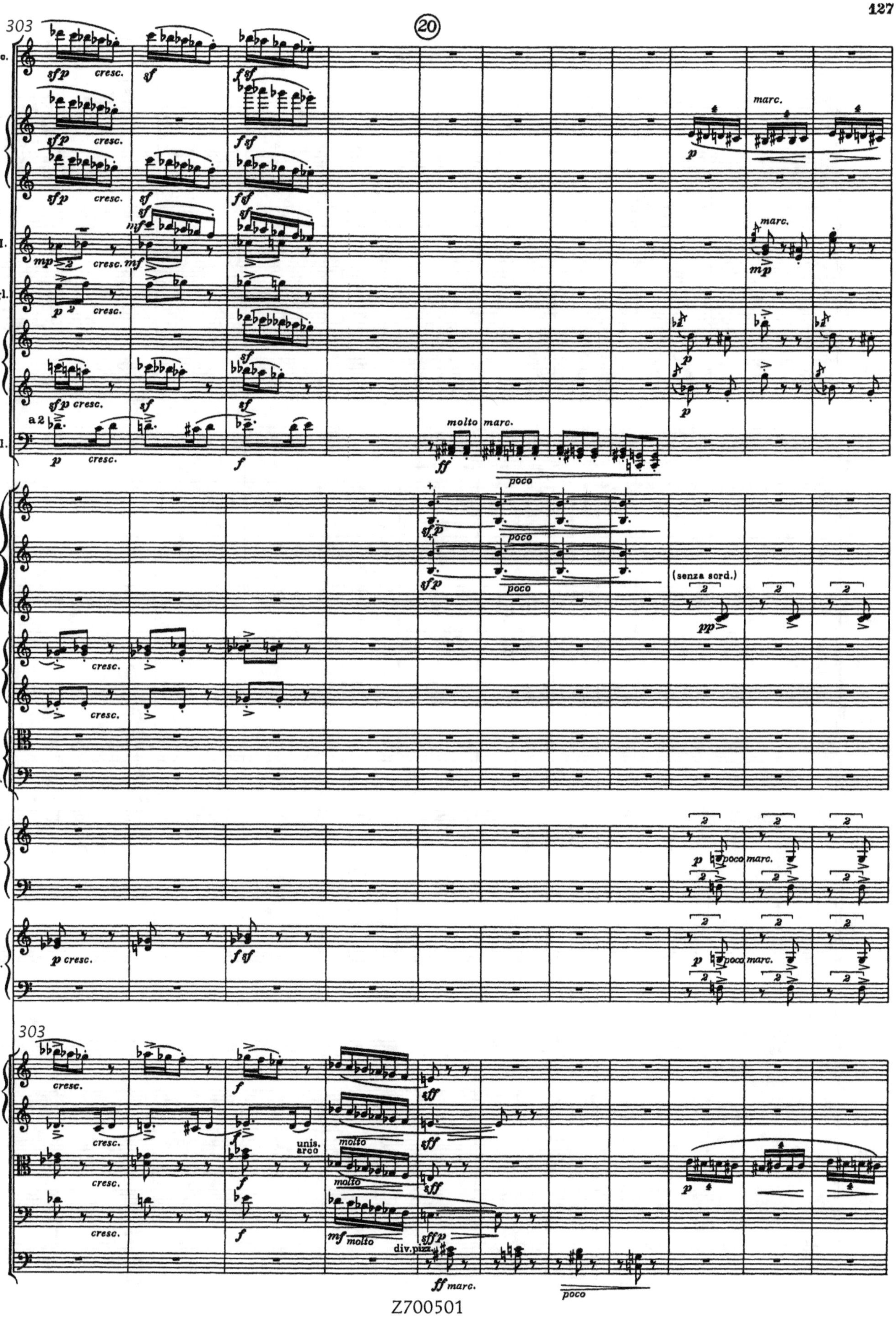
303
20
Fl. picc.
I.
Fl.
II.
Ob. I. II.
Cor. ingl.
I.
Cl. A
II.
Fag. I. II.
a 2
molto marc.
poco
I. II.
Cor. F III. IV.
V. VI.
(senza sord.)
I. II.
Trbe C
III.
I. II.
Trbni
III. e Tb.
Arpa I.
Arpa II.
poco marc.
303
I.
Viol.
II.
Vle
Vlc.
Cb.
cresc.
marc.
unis.
arco
molto
div. pizz.
ff marc.

356
Fl. I. II.
Ob. I. II.
Cl. I. II. A
Cl. basso A
Fag. I. II.
Cfag.
a 2
ten.
I. II.
Cor. F
III. IV.
Trbe I. II. C
I. II.
Trbni
III. e Tb.
Timp.
356
I.
Viol.
II.
Vle
Vlc.
Cb.

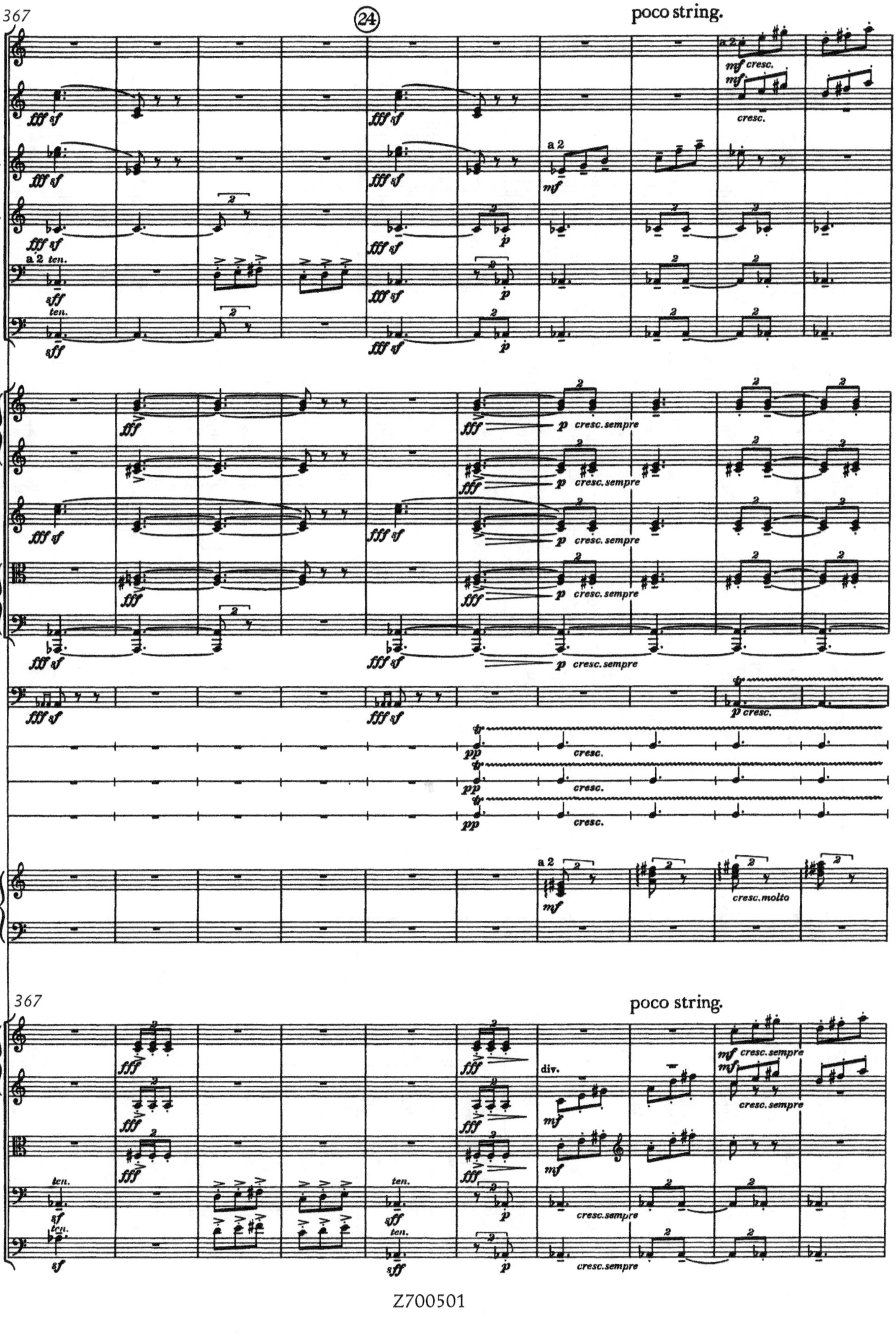
367
24
poco string.
Fl. I. II.
Ob. I. II.
Cl. I. II. A
Cl. basso A
Fag. I. II.
Cfag.
I. II. Cor. F III. IV.
Trbe I. II. C
I. II. Trbni III. e Tb.
Timp.
Trgl.
Piatti
Gr. C.
Arpe I. II.
367
poco string.
I. Viol. II.
Vle
Vlc.
Cb.
a 2 ten.
a 2
div.
cresc.
cresc. sempre
cresc. molto

148

150

153

154

158

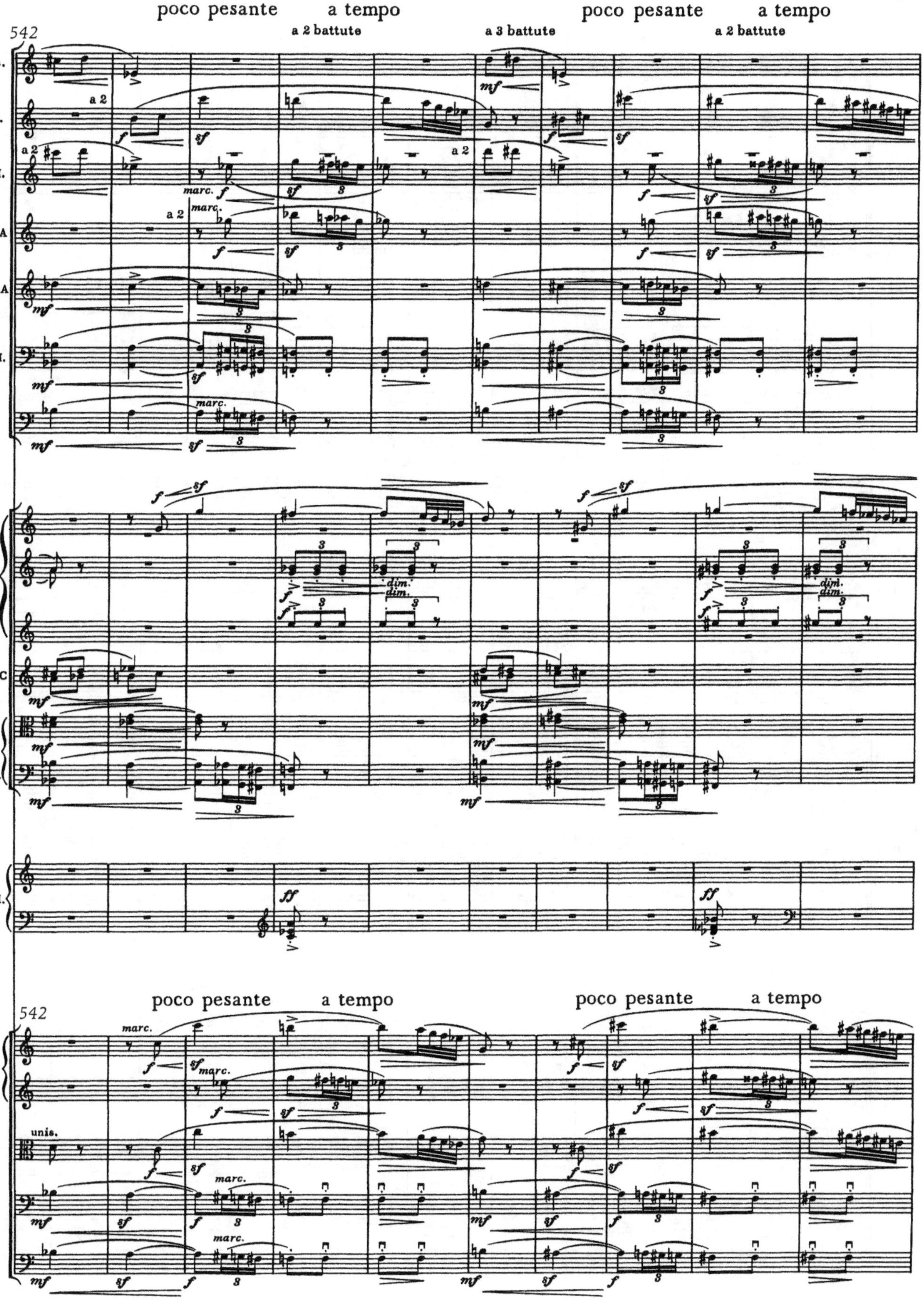
542
poco pesante
a tempo
a 2 battute
a 3 battute
a 2 battute
Fl. picc.
Fl. I. II.
Ob. I. II.
Cl. I. II. A
Cl. basso A
Fag. I. II.
Cfag.
a 2
marc.
I. II.
Cor. III. IV. F
V. VI.
dim.
Trbe I. II. C
I. II.
Trbni
III. e Tb.
Arpe I., II.
I.
Viol.
II.
unis.
Vle
Vlc.
Cb.

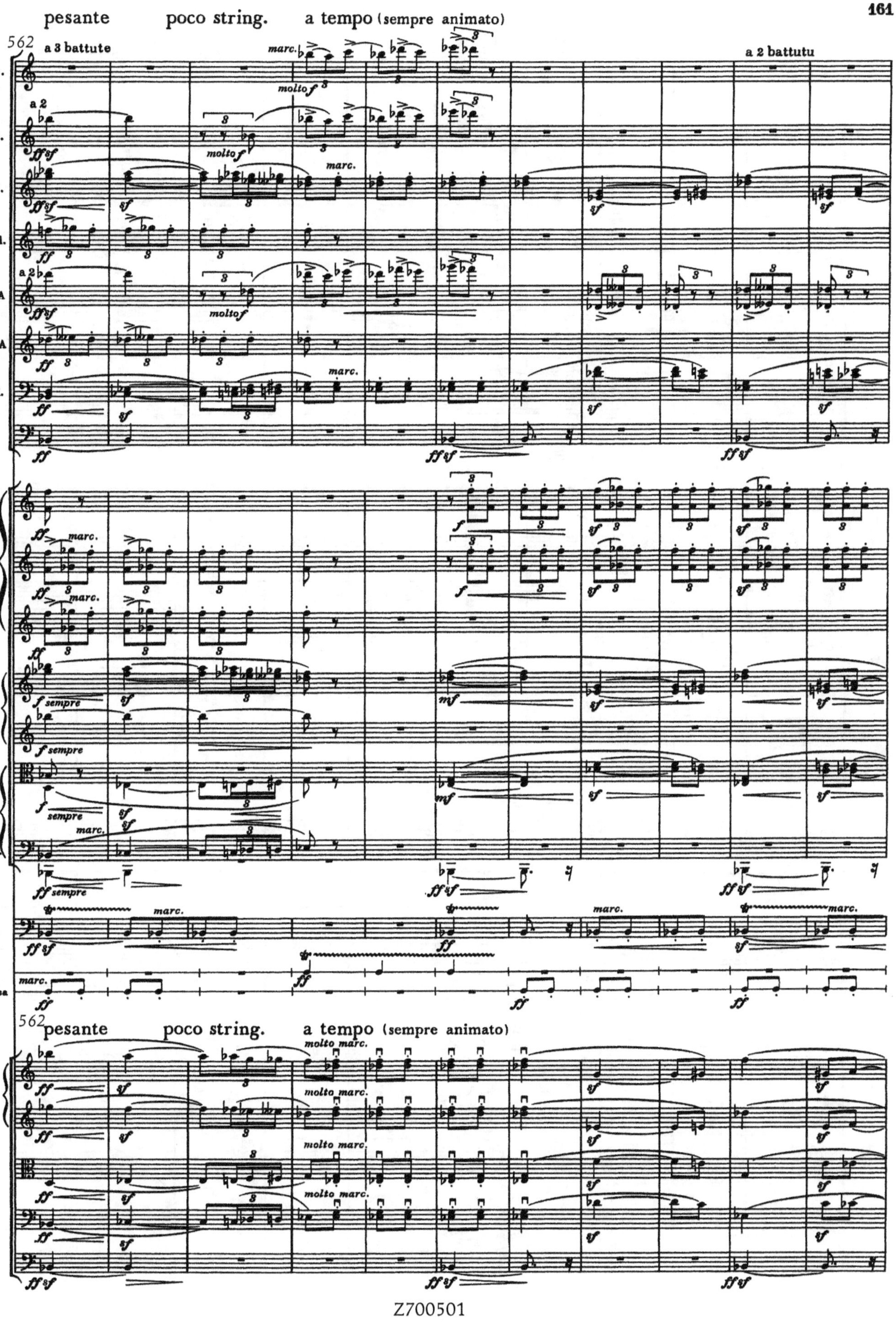
pesante poco string. a tempo (sempre animato)
562
a 3 battute
a 2 battutu
Fl. picc.
Fl. I. II.
Ob. I. II.
Cor. ingl.
Cl. I. II. A
Cl. basso A
Fag. I. II.
Cfag.
Cor. III. IV. F
V. VI.
Trbe C
Trbni
III. e Tb.
Timp.
Trgl.
Gr. Cassa
Viol.
Vle
Vlc.
Cb.
marc.
molto f
molto marc.
f sempre
sempre

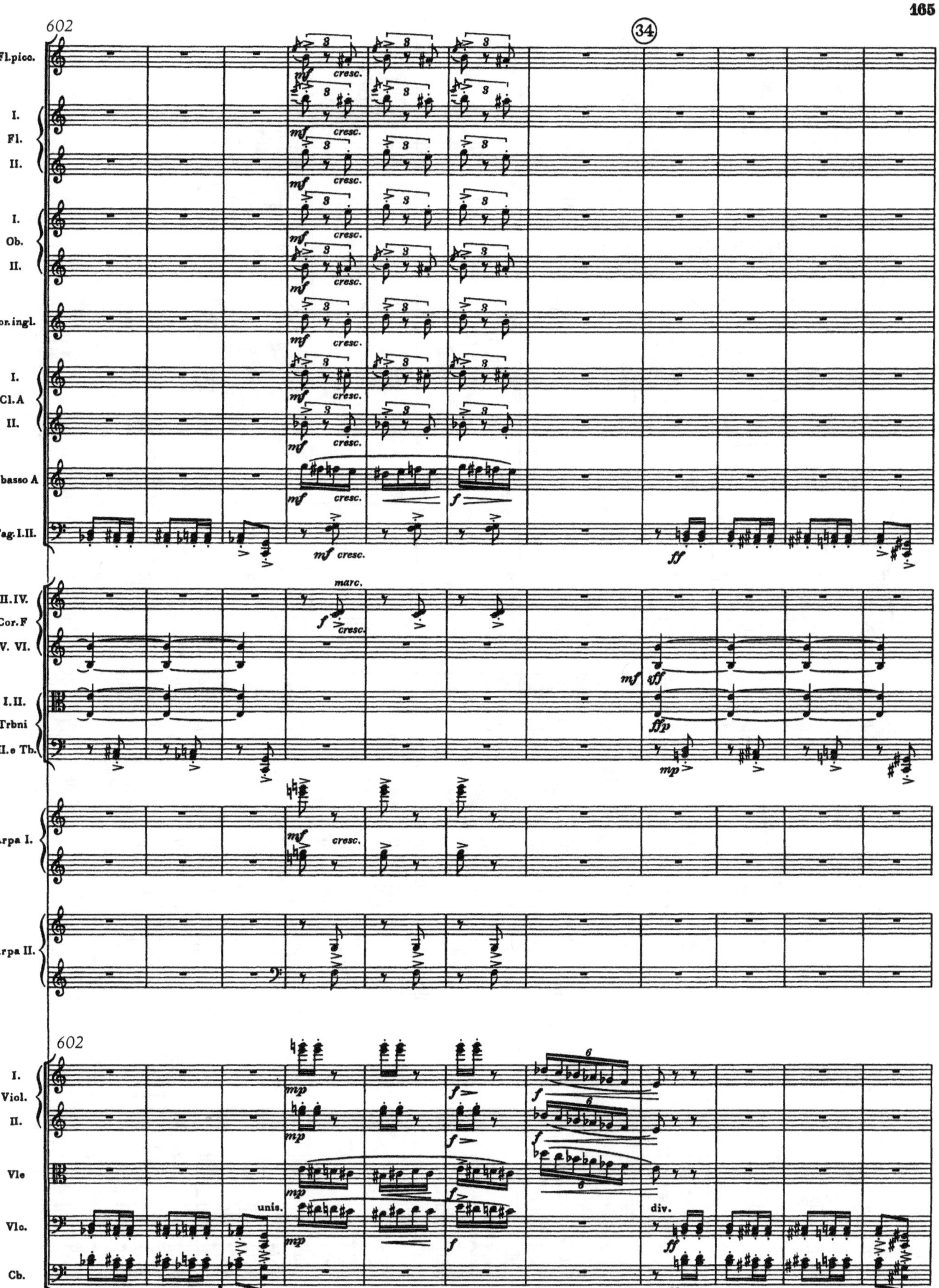
602
34
Fl.picc.
I. Fl. II.
I. Ob. II.
Cor. ingl.
I. Cl. A II.
Cl. basso A
Fag. I. II.
III. IV. Cor. F V. VI.
I. II. Trbni III. e Tb.
Arpa I.
Arpa II.
I. Viol. II.
Vle
Vlc.
Cb.
mf
cresc.
marc.
f
ff
sff
ffp
mp
unis.
div.

V. Noc
(Night)

178

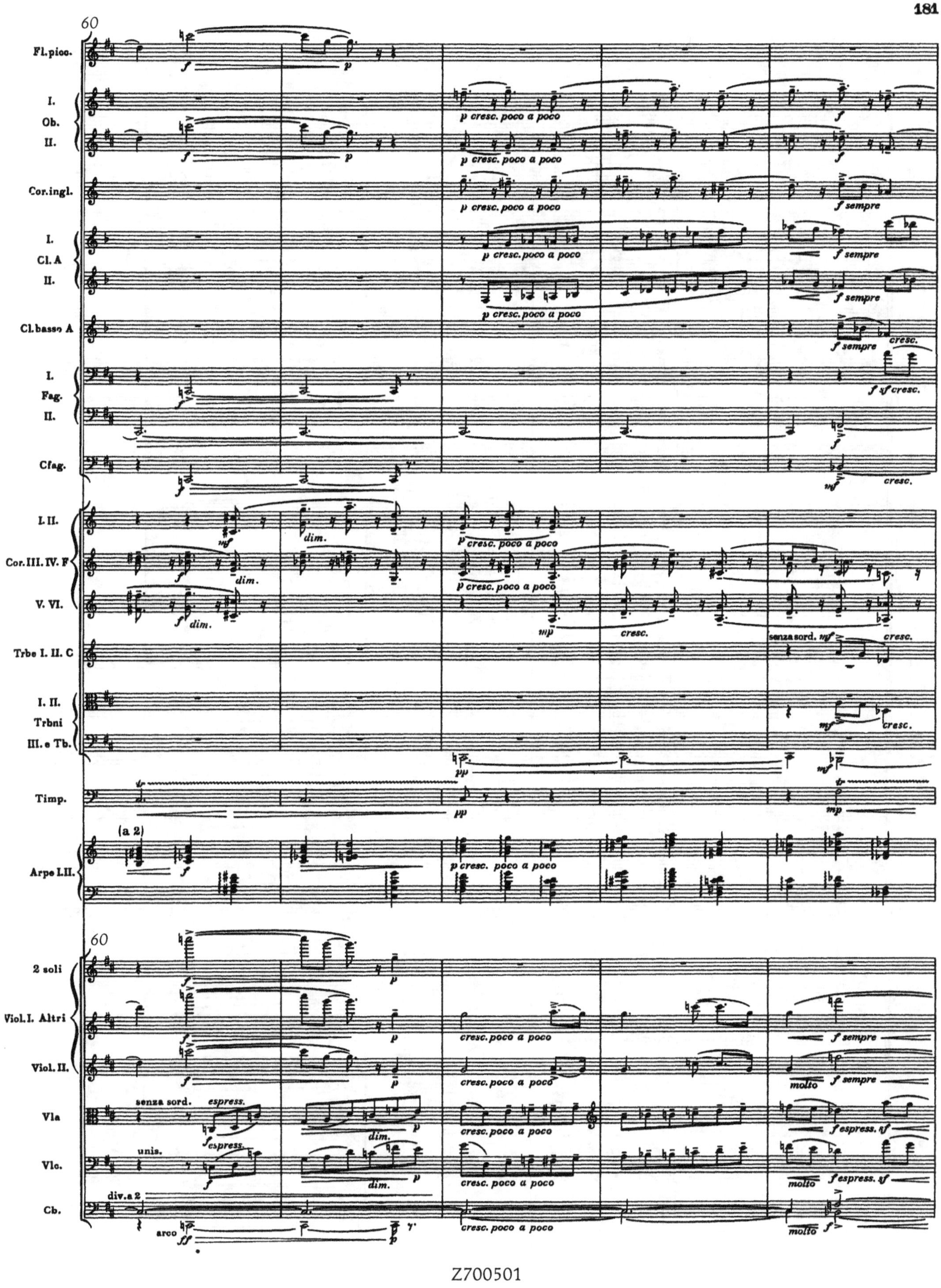
60
Fl. picc.
I. Ob. II.
Cor. ingl.
I. Cl. A II.
Cl. basso A
I. Fag. II.
Cfag.
I. II.
Cor. III. IV. F
V. VI.
Trbe I. II. C
I. II. Trbni III. e Tb.
Timp.
(a 2)
Arpe I. II.
60
2 soli
Viol. I. Altri
Viol. II.
Vla
Vlc.
Cb.
p cresc. poco a poco
f sempre
dim.
mf
cresc.
senza sord.
espress.
unis.
div. a 2
arco
molto
f espress. sf
cresc. poco a poco

*) Respirare di rado e solltanto a terzo quarto

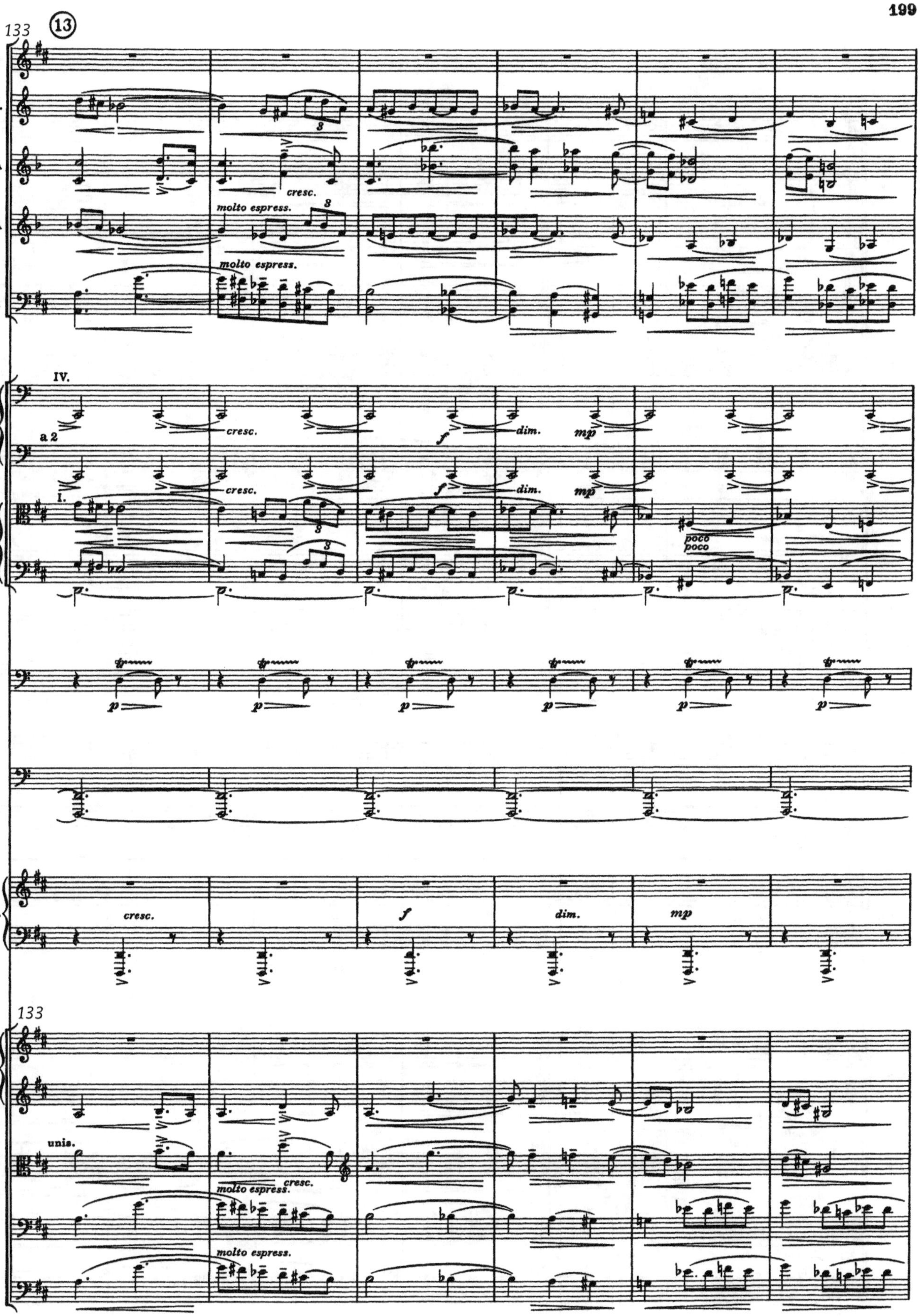
133
13
Fl. I. II.
Cor. ingl.
Cl. I. II. A
cresc.
Cl. basso A
molto espress.
Fag. I. II.
molto espress.
IV.
IV.
Cor. D
a 2
V. VI.
cresc.
f
dim.
mp
I.
I.
Trbni
III. e Tb.
poco
poco
Timp.
p
Org.
Arpe I., II.
cresc.
f
dim.
mp
133
I.
Viol.
II.
unis.
Vle
molto espress.
cresc.
Vlc.
molto espress.
Cb.

204

*) Può riprendere il flauto grande

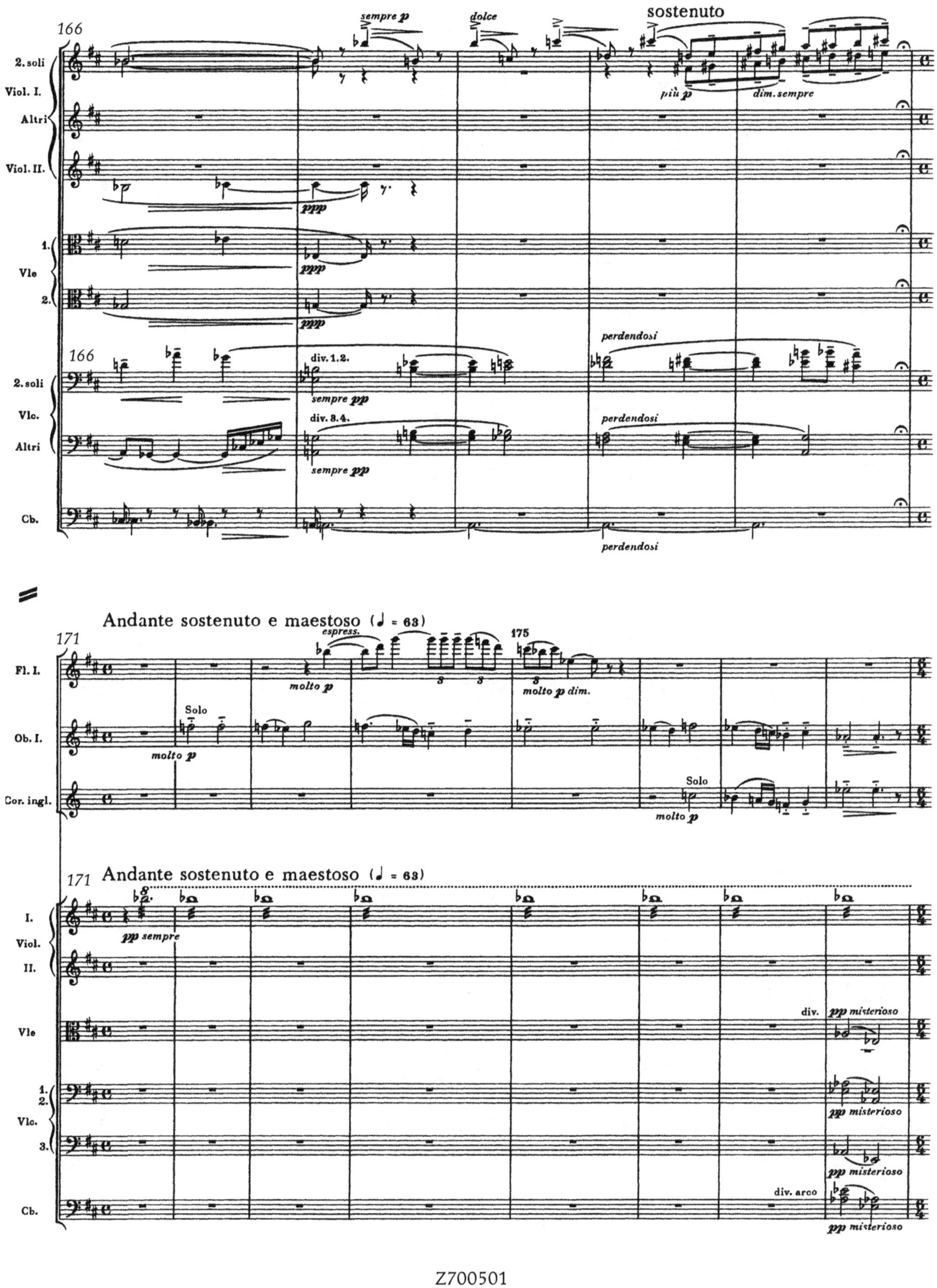
166
sostenuto
2. soli
Viol. I.
Altri
Viol. II.
Vle
Vlc.
Cb.
sempre p
dolce
più p
dim. sempre
ppp
div. 1.2.
sempre pp
div. 3.4.
perdendosi
Andante sostenuto e maestoso (♩ = 63)
171
175
Fl. I.
Ob. I.
Cor. ingl.
Solo
espress.
molto p
molto p dim.
pp sempre
div.
pp misterioso
div. arco

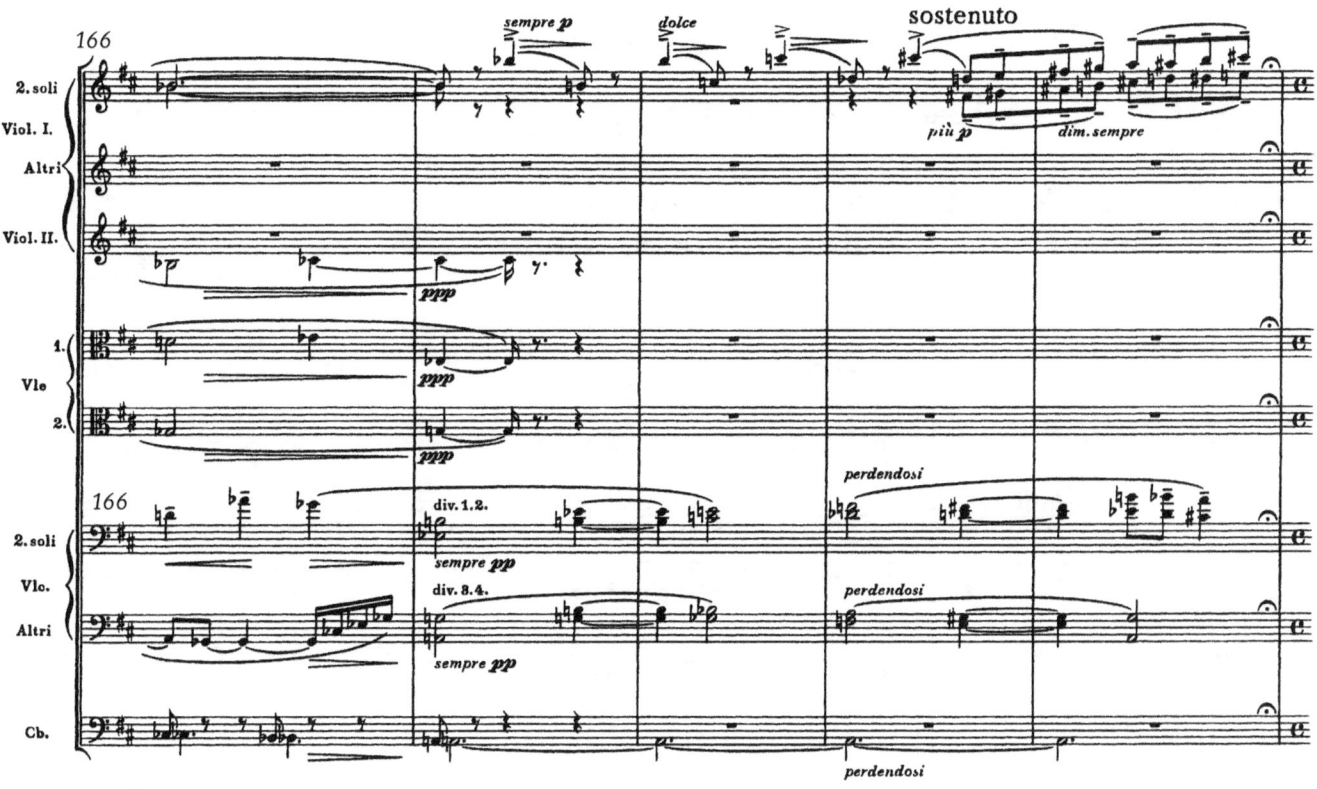

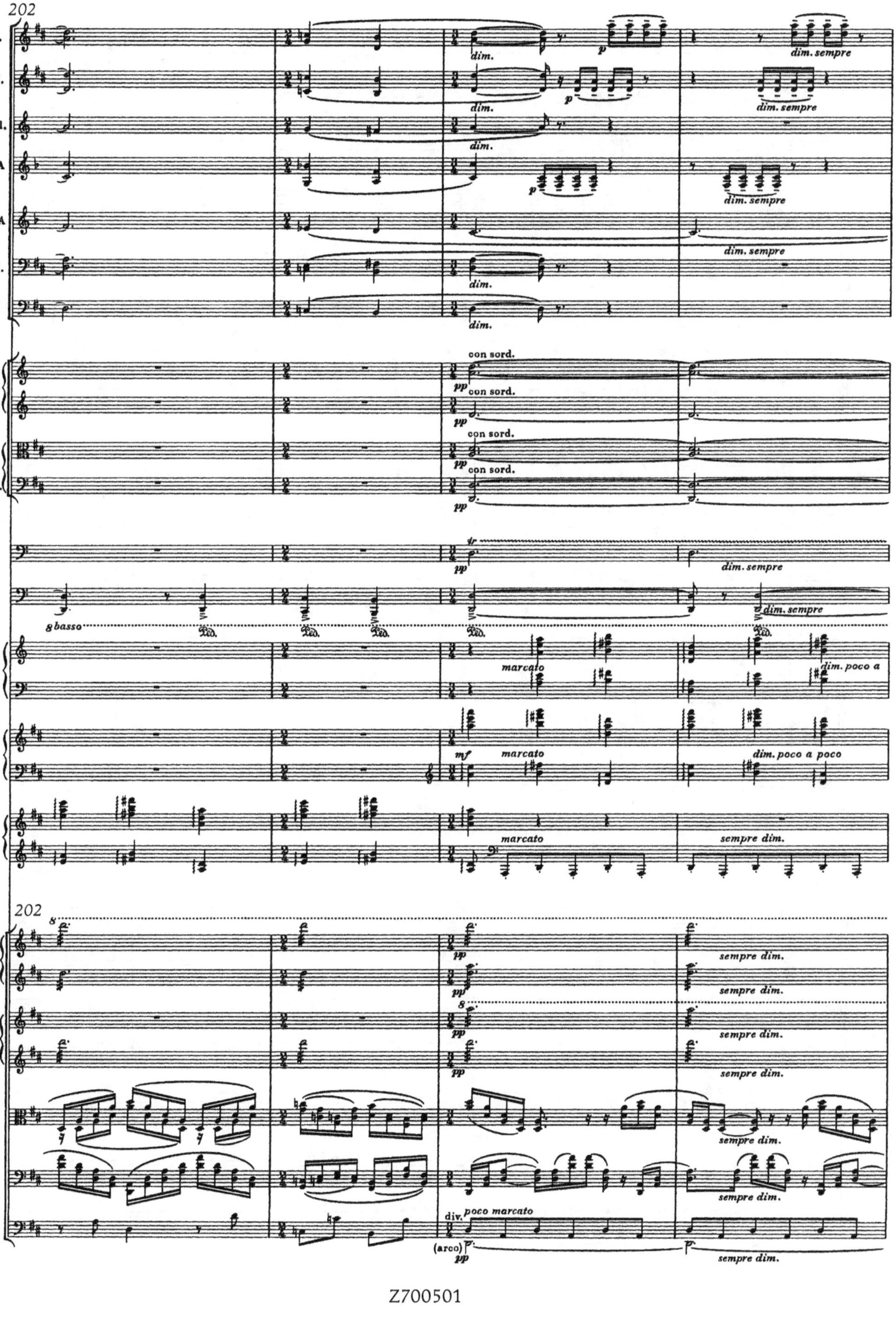
202
Fl. I. II.
Ob. I. II.
Cor. ingl.
Cl. I. II. A
Cl. basso A
Fag. I. II.
Cfag.
I. II.
Trbe C
III.
I. II.
Trbni
III. e Tb.
Timp.
Pianof.
Celesta
Arpa I.
Arpa II.
Viol. I.
Viol. II.
Vle
Vlc.
Cb.
dim.
p
dim. sempre
con sord.
pp
tr
8 basso
marcato
mf
dim. poco a
dim. poco a poco
sempre dim.
poco marcato
div.
(arco)

www.ingramcontent.com/pod-product-compliance
Lightning Source LLC
Chambersburg PA
CBHW082119230426
43671CB00015B/2745